Coop's
day at the park!

DiseñoGráfico - Nit 700031049 © Marta Recaredo P. 2023

ISBN: 9798375551401

Do you like parks? I love them!
I love parks and everything I can do when I go to one.
I can play games with my friends, run around, fly kites
or play ball. Visit the little animals that live there or
oook inside the trees or the nests in the trees. The anthills
are my favorites. They are amazing! Did you know some of
the seeds they use to build their homes later grow to be the
flowers and also the big trees at the park?The flowers feed
the birds and the bees and the trees grow so big we can
sit under their branches and have a picnic.
Let's go to the park!

We are going on a picnic!

Ela was very happy because they were going
to spend the day at the park and have a picnic.
She woke up early and rushed to wake everybody up!
-Come on mom, dad, Ribbit, Coop! Is time to go!
She was very excited.As they were leaving the house
mom overheard Ela saying:-" Dad, the snacks. Don't
forget them!"-Mom smiled:- Come on Ela! Lets go.We
got it. We are ready to go. Dad grinned and winked
at them, -Yes, kiddo, we got everything. Lets go!
On their way to the car Ela was very excited she was
singing -" We are having a picnic ♫♫ We are going
on a picnic ♫♫♫Our day is going to be fantastic ♫♫♫ "
They got in the car and drove for a little while until they
arrived at a beautiful park outside the city.

As soon as the car was parked, Ela grabbed
Coop and Ribbit, opened the door and jumped out
of the car to look for the perfect spot for their picnic.
-Let's go Coop, Let's go Ribbit!
She was running all over the place as her parents
were carrying the basket out of the trunk.
Mom grinned while her eyes twitched.
-Ela! Don't go far. Please, wait for us.

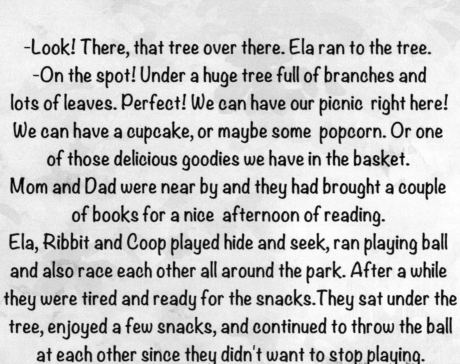

-Look! There, that tree over there. Ela ran to the tree.
-On the spot! Under a huge tree full of branches and
lots of leaves. Perfect! We can have our picnic right here!
We can have a cupcake, or maybe some popcorn. Or one
of those delicious goodies we have in the basket.
Mom and Dad were near by and they had brought a couple
of books for a nice afternoon of reading.
Ela, Ribbit and Coop played hide and seek, ran playing ball
and also race each other all around the park. After a while
they were tired and ready for the snacks.They sat under the
tree, enjoyed a few snacks, and continued to throw the ball
at each other since they didn't want to stop playing.

The ball flew over Coop's head. He stood up and ran after the ball. — I got it! I got it!

Ela saw there was a piece of trunk covered with grass a few steps from Coop and tried to warn him.

He tripped over the trunk covered in grass.
Coop flew through the air doing somersaults
and when he landed on the grass he rolled
away even further from Ela and Ribbit.
After a few more laps he landed on his back.

-Coop! Cooooooop! Where are you?

Ela grabbed Ribbit
- Let's go! We have to help him!

The ants at the park heard a loud noise very close to them. They took off to find out what had happened. They didn't waste any time when they saw Coop on the ground. One of the ants grabbed a large leaf and turned it into a megaphone , inmediately calling for help.

As soon as he opened his eyes
he saw lots of ants around him but he didn't quite
understood what was happening. Cooper heard some
very soft and strange little voices around him whispering :

-"It's a bear! Yes! it is a teddy bear." Coop was dizzy
and was still trying to understand what had happened
or where he was. He wondered where Ela and Ribbit were.

Ants gather around him.
They were very curious and wanted to
know what had happened to him.

Poor Coop he looked awful.
He had scratches all over his body and was
covered with bruises.

The firetruck, the Red Cross ambulance and a helicopter arrived. The ants jumped running while waving their arms. All of them! As soon as the rescuers saw the ants they followed them.

The sound of the fire truck, ambulance, and helicopter sirens signaled that Coop would soon receive the help he needed. The rescuers were fully equipped and ready to land. The firetruck followed the pathway of leaves on the grass.

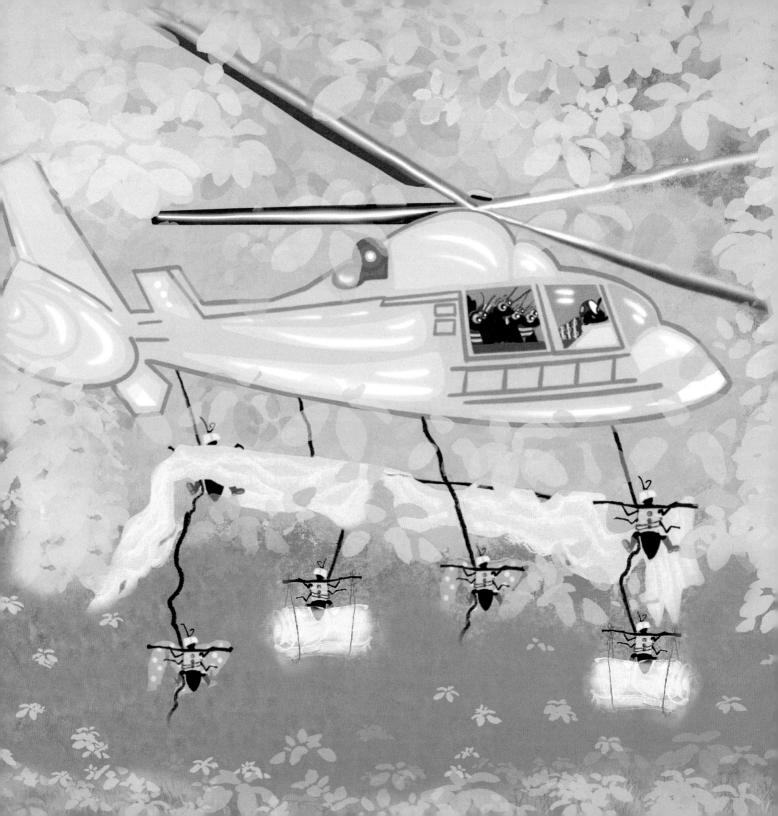

The ambulance arrived loaded with everything to heal Coop's wounds. Bandages, stiches and medicines. But they were going to need lots of help from everybody because Coop was really BIG!

Poor Coop felt lightheaded and a little lost. He heard Ela calling him from a distance, but he soon dozed off. The firefighters opened the waterhose and that was the last thing Coop heard.

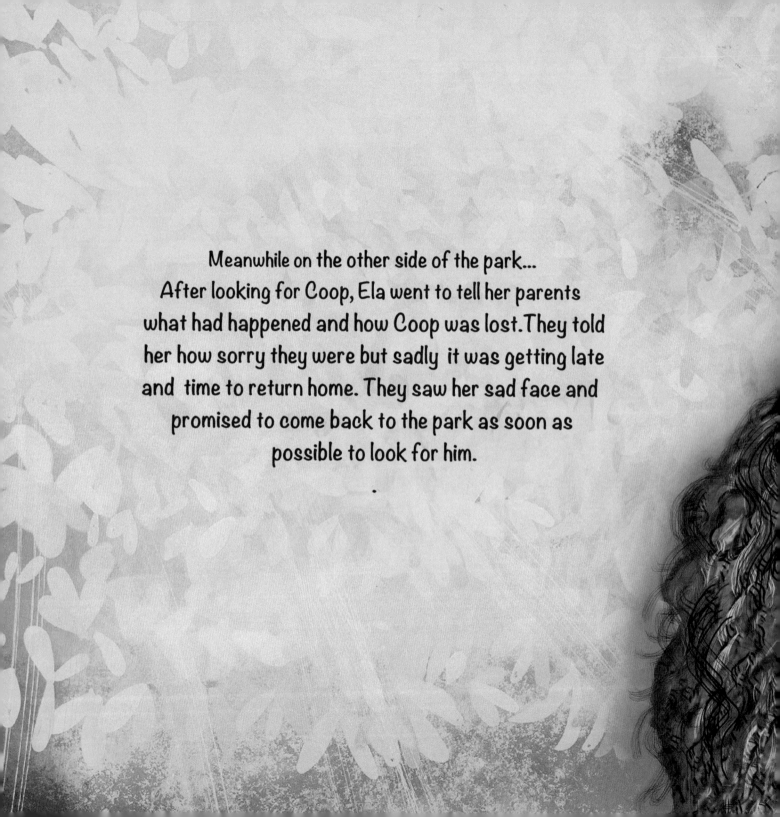

Meanwhile on the other side of the park...
After looking for Coop, Ela went to tell her parents
what had happened and how Coop was lost. They told
her how sorry they were but sadly it was getting late
and time to return home. They saw her sad face and
promised to come back to the park as soon as
possible to look for him.

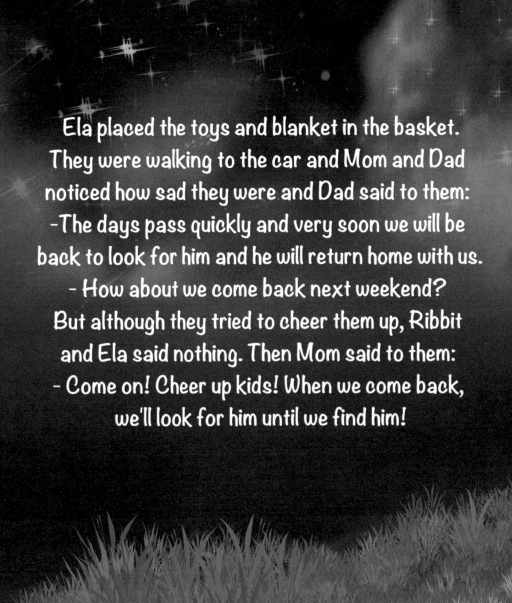

Ela placed the toys and blanket in the basket.
They were walking to the car and Mom and Dad
noticed how sad they were and Dad said to them:
-The days pass quickly and very soon we will be
back to look for him and he will return home with us.
- How about we come back next weekend?
But although they tried to cheer them up, Ribbit
and Ela said nothing. Then Mom said to them:
- Come on! Cheer up kids! When we come back,
we'll look for him until we find him!

Ela rolled down the window and kept staring at the
sky remembering her grandma had told her how stars
can make wishes come true.She had to look out for
the brightest star, not necessarily the biggest but the
brightest and make her wish. Then all she had to do
is wait. She found the brightest star and whispered:
" Next time we come to the park I want to find Coop
and bring him home. Please make my wish come true"

The next day at the park the morning was sunny and warm. The word spread fast and there were more and more ants going to see the big teddy bear to check on his recovery. They loved the idea of having a new friend and were super nice to him. Coop was feeling a bit better and was very happy to have so many new friends.He was enjoying the attention very much.They invited him to walk around the park oncehe felt better.They wanted to show him where their homes and also play a few games.

As soon as he felt better, he got up and went to find his new friends. The place was great. They even had a swimming pool and played lots of games in the park. There were fruits everywhere! Colorful strawberries and cherries. He felt a delicious aroma and his nose lead him to a small pipe on the ground. He took a peek inside and saw mama ant's kitchen. She was preparing a delicious meal. The smell reminded him of home. And just as he was starting to get homesick, he heard his friends...

They all went to play PineCone-Ball.
It was very much like a football game but the ball was a pine cone.
There were two teams and this time of the teams had more ants
than the other because Coop was a lot bigger and stronger.

All the ants were cheering for Coop:
Kick it hard Coop.Way to go Coop!
Hip-Hip Hurray for Coop!

Hip-Hip Hurray for Coop!

After the game, the ants invited him to walk around the park. His new friends were always busy doing something. There were so many fruits on the grass and not only they ate them but also played with them. They new how to have fun! They ran around the park and some of them had their floaters on ready to jump in the pool.

Coop leaned forward and enjoyed the kites flying their way up to the clouds. He felt something tickle on his face. He was about to scratch his cheek when he heard something

– Wait coop wait! It's me! Itchy,I called the rescuers to help you.
Coop barely remembered it, but he remembered his voice

Itchy jumped on Coop's hand
-Coop today is my birthday and we are having a party!
Would you like to come and celebrate with us?
Surprised and very happy for the invitation,
he accepted right away!

On their way to the party, Coop and friends heard:
-Coooooper! Coop! where are you?Where are you buddy?
Coop inmediately recognized Ela's voice and followed it.
Only took them a few steps to see each other again.They
hugged very tight. Ela had a present for Coop. A box full
of gummies and candy. As soon as he saw the candy he
screamed: -Jellybeans! My favorites! Also told them all
about his new friends and the party. He wanted them to
join him to meet his new friends.: -Sure Coop! -Would
you like to give your friend the box of candies as a
birthday present?And she whispered to his ear:
-We have lots of them at home waiting just for you.
Coop looked at Ribbit 's ears flipping up and down at
the sametime he winked at him. Coop hugged them.
- Thank you! Let's go.

Let's party! The band was playing and
all the ants brought lots of food and presents

I want the green!
Ok,ok! let me grab it !
I love pink!
Come on guys help me put it down!
I got mine! Hurray!

They were having so much fun that they lost
track of time when suddenly they heard mom
and dad calling out . - Ela, Coop and Ribbit
time to go! They all got a bit sad because they
didn't want to say good bye but she promised
to them they would be back pretty soon to have
another picnic. Ela grabbed Coop and Ribbit
and ran to the car. Mom and dad were waiting
for them with the car doors opened. When they
saw Coop they gave him a big hug. Mom asked :
- Are we ready to go back home?
- Yes mom! Let's go!
As they drove away they saw the ants running
after the car waving goodbye.

Made in the USA
Middletown, DE
19 March 2023